Race Car Crew Chief

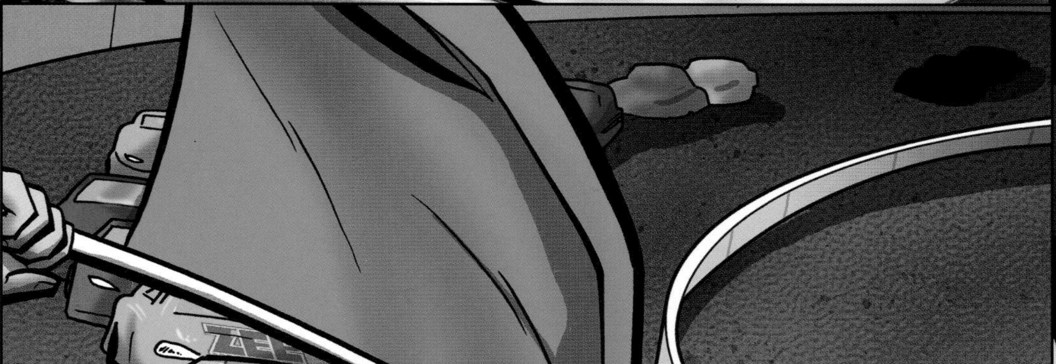
ARROW
62
Norman
32
SOS

By Susan Koehler
Illustrated By Thomas Zahler

Rourke Publishing
Vero Beach, Florida 32964

www.rourkepublishing.com

Edited by Meg Greve
Illustrated by Thomas Zahler
Art Direction and Page Layout by Renee Brady

Photo Credits: © Brian Cantoni: page 26; © Random Photography: page 27; © Arlo Abrahamson: page 27; © National Guard: page 28

Library of Congress Cataloging-in-Publication Data

Koehler, Susan, 1963-
  Race car crew chief / Susan Koehler.
     p. cm. -- (Jobs that rock graphic illustrated)
  Includes bibliographical references and index.
  ISBN 978-1-60694-375-5 (alk. paper)
  ISBN 978-1-60694-558-2 (soft cover)
 1. Pit crews--Comic books, strips, etc. 2. Pit crews--Vocational guidance--Juvenile literature.
Title.
  GV1029+

                              2009020485

Printed in the USA
CG/CG

www.rourkepublishing.com - rourke@rourkepublishing.com
Post Office Box 643328 Vero Beach, Florida 32964

Table of Contents

Sally Nash

Sally Nash is a 10-year-old girl who wants to meet her favorite NASCAR driver.

Mr. and Mrs. Nash

Mr. and Mrs. Nash are Sally's parents.

Dirk Durham

Dirk Durham is a race car driver who wants to win.

J.B. Clifton

J.B. Clifton is Dirk Durham's race car crew chief.

CHAPTER 1

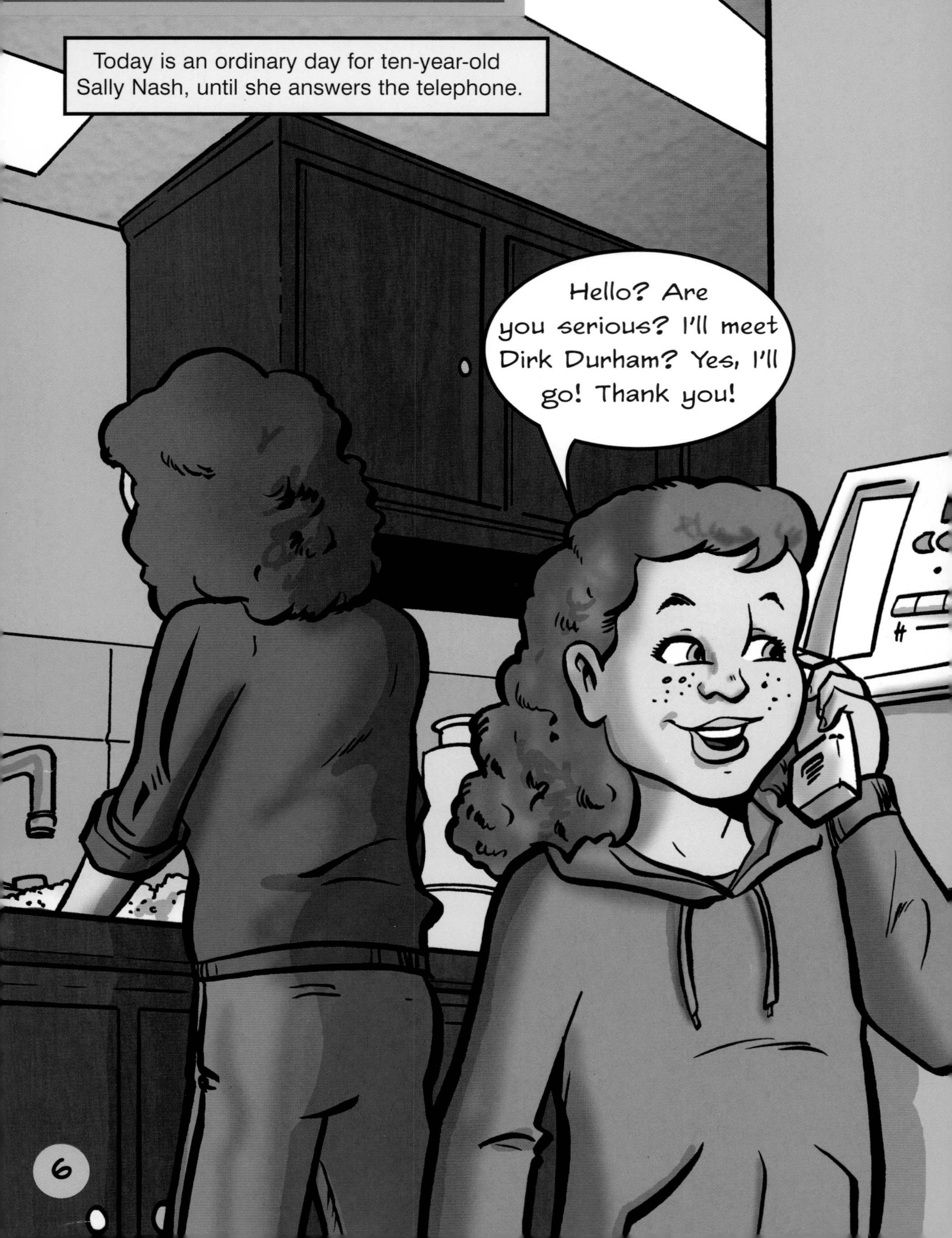
Today is an ordinary day for ten-year-old Sally Nash, until she answers the telephone.
Hello? Are you serious? I'll meet Dirk Durham? Yes, I'll go! Thank you!

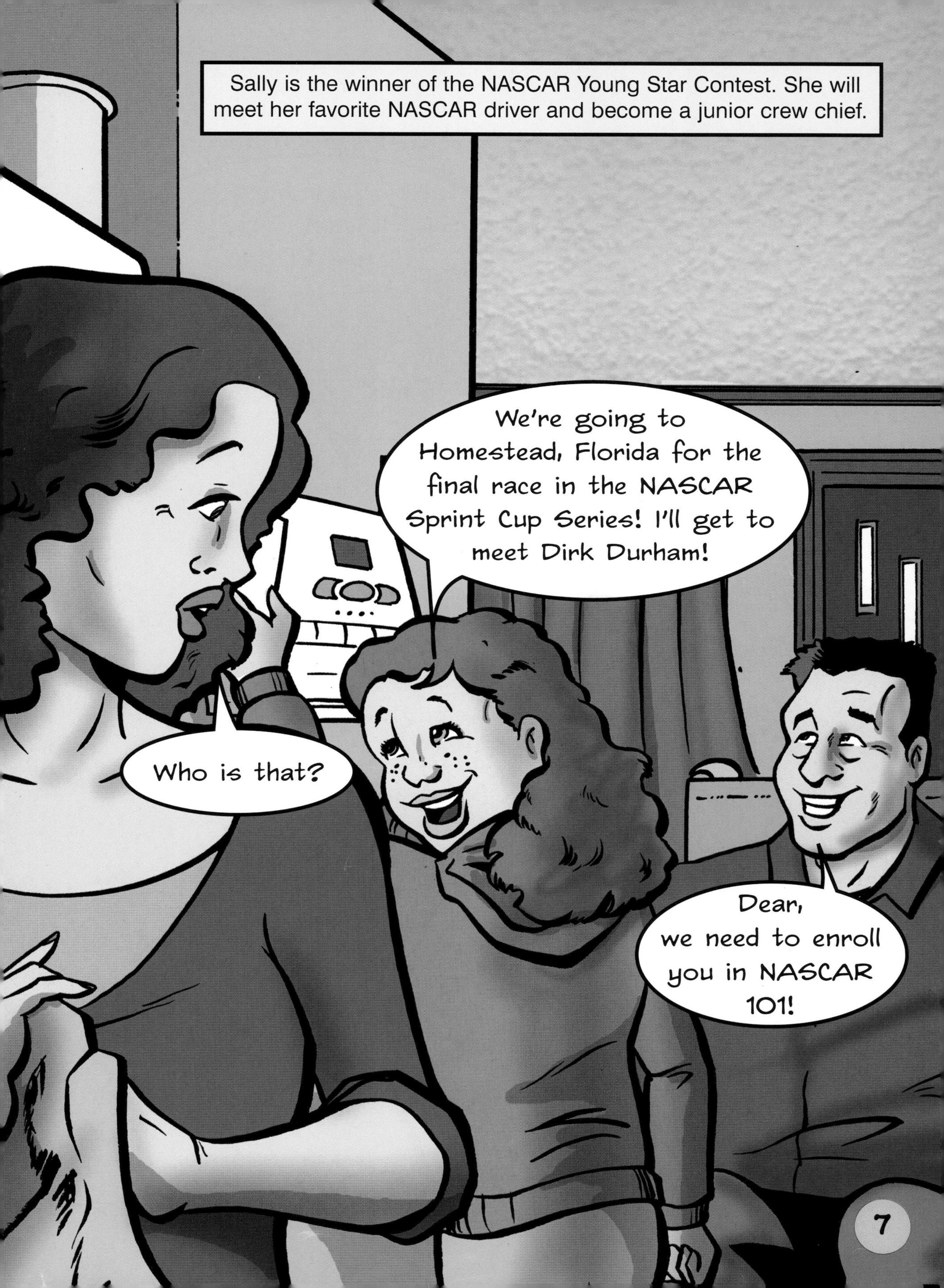
Sally is the winner of the NASCAR Young Star Contest. She will meet her favorite NASCAR driver and become a junior crew chief.
We're going to Homestead, Florida for the final race in the NASCAR Sprint Cup Series! I'll get to meet Dirk Durham!
Who is that?
Dear, we need to enroll you in NASCAR 101!

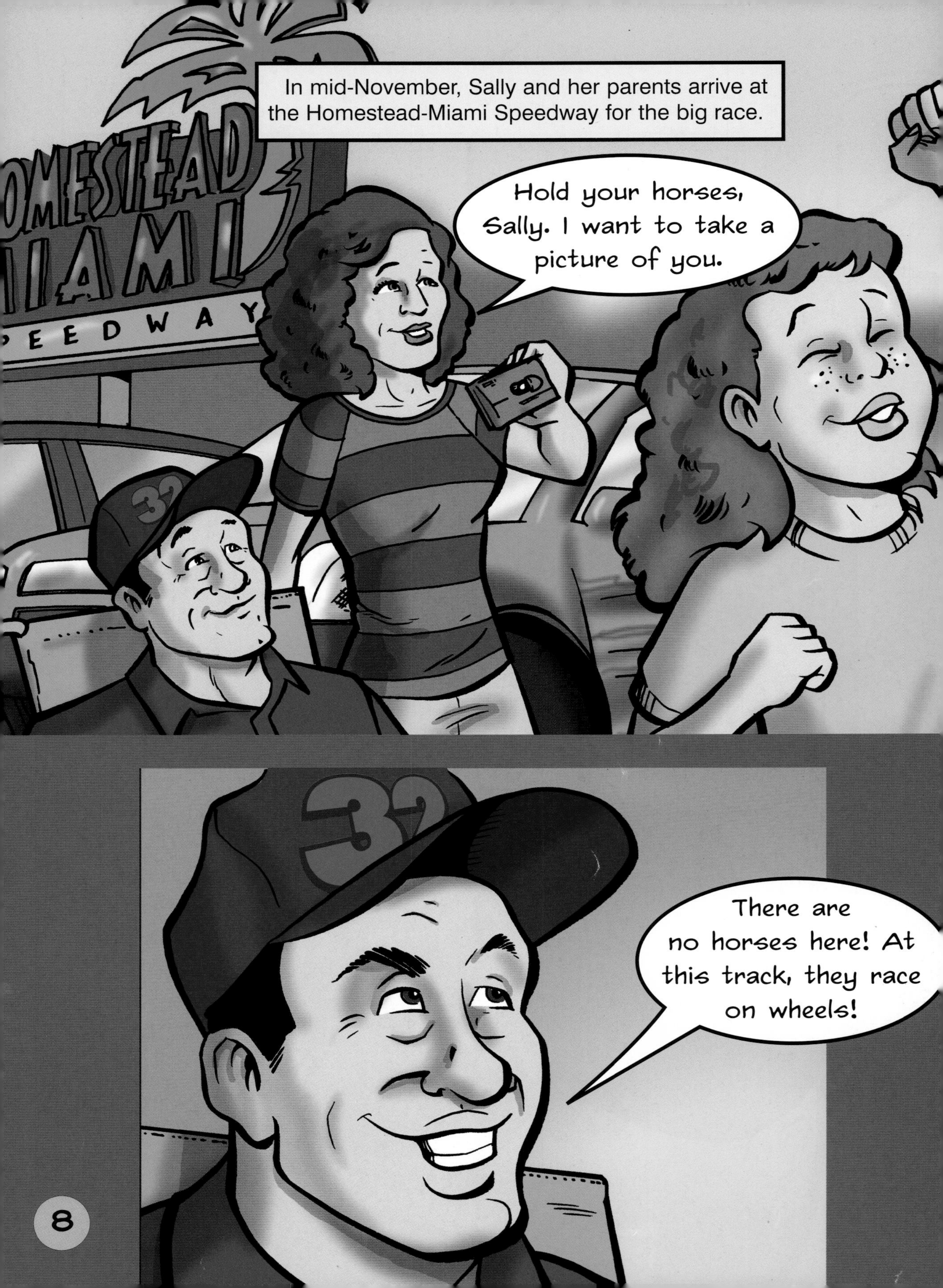
In mid-November, Sally and her parents arrive at the Homestead-Miami Speedway for the big race.
HOMESTEAD MIAMI SPEEDWAY
Hold your horses, Sally. I want to take a picture of you.
There are no horses here! At this track, they race on wheels!

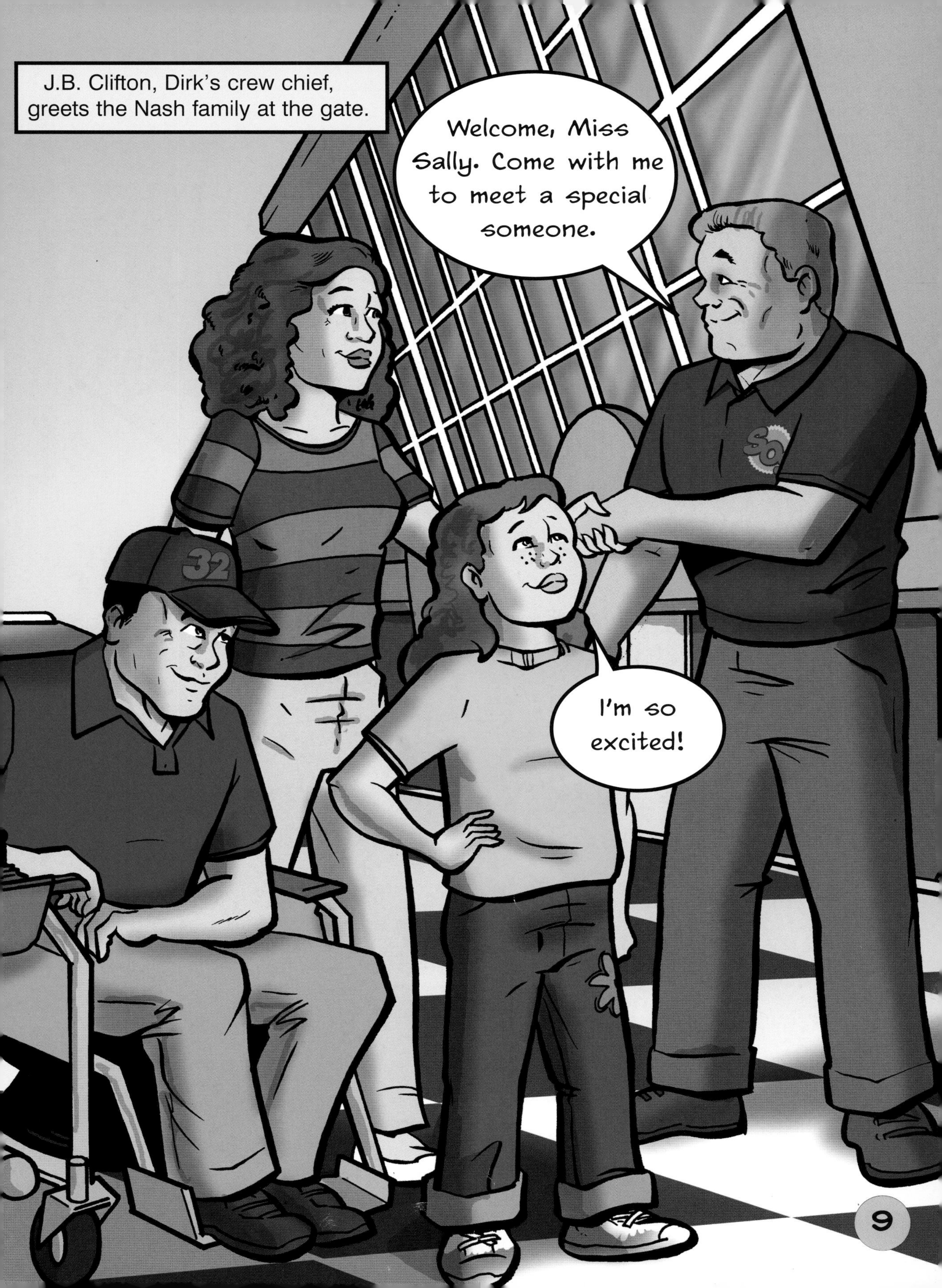
J.B. Clifton, Dirk's crew chief, greets the Nash family at the gate.
Welcome, Miss Sally. Come with me to meet a special someone.
I'm so excited!
32

CHAPTER 2

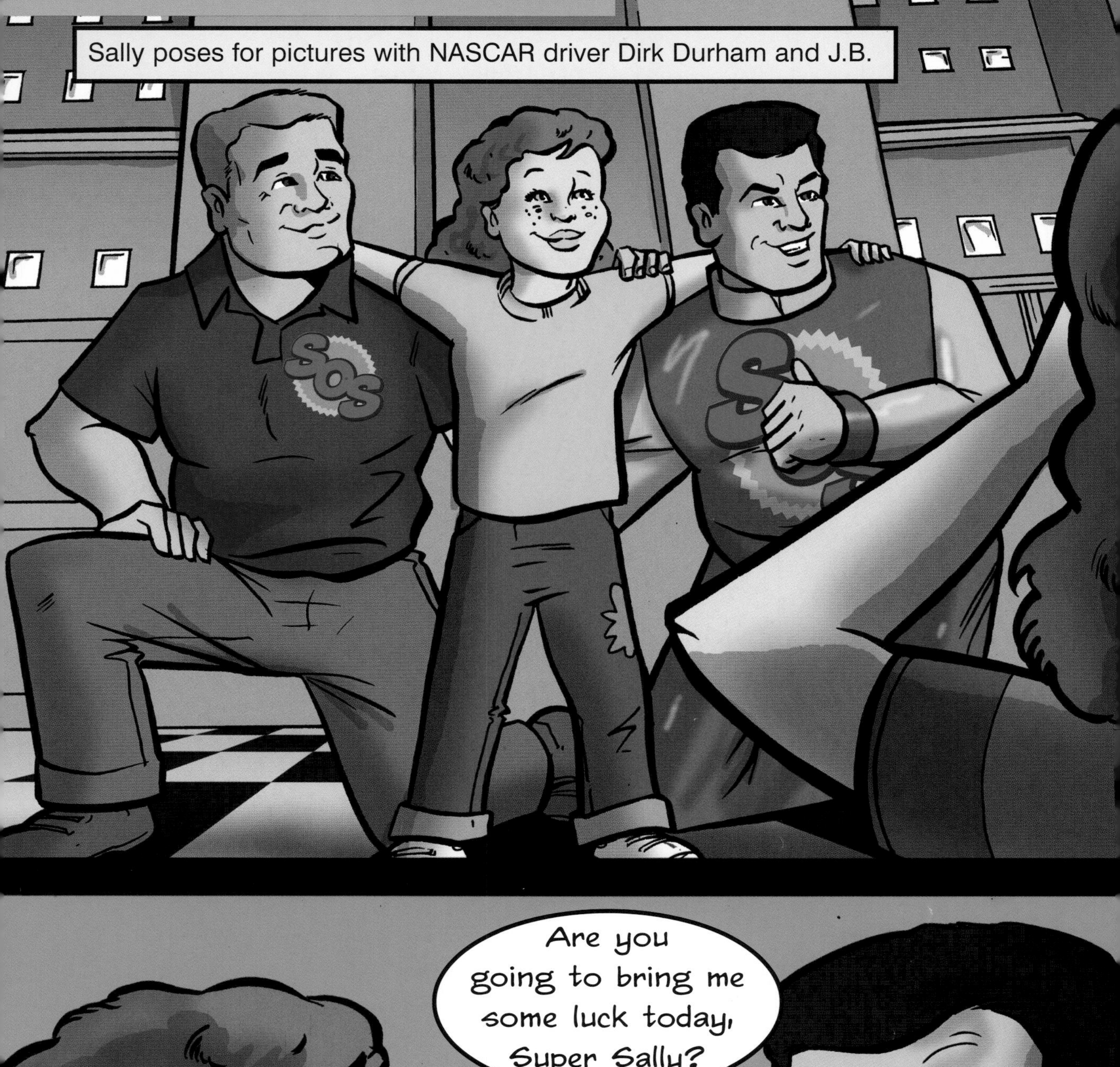
Sally poses for pictures with NASCAR driver Dirk Durham and J.B.
SOS

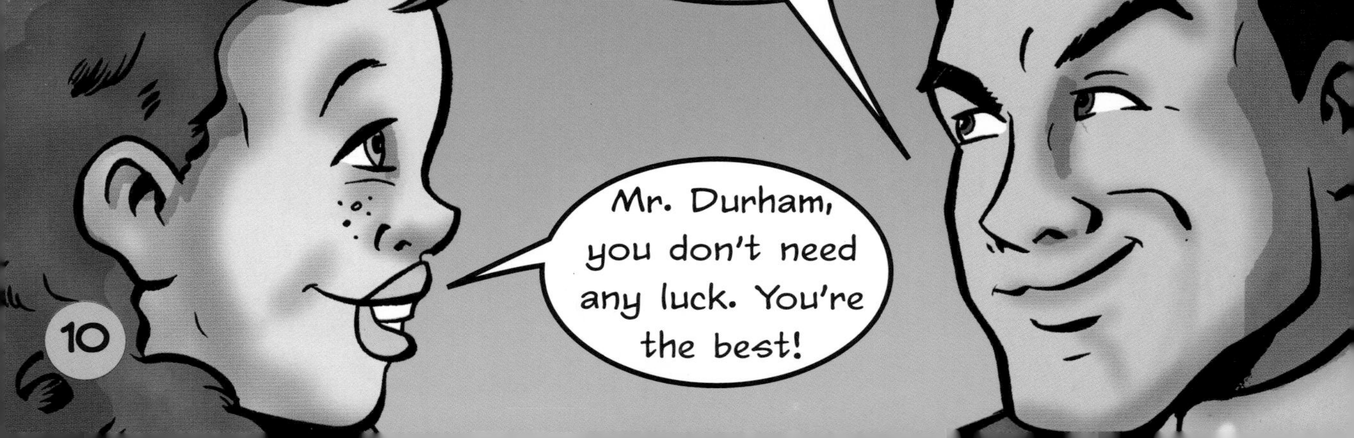
Are you going to bring me some luck today, Super Sally?
Mr. Durham, you don't need any luck. You're the best!

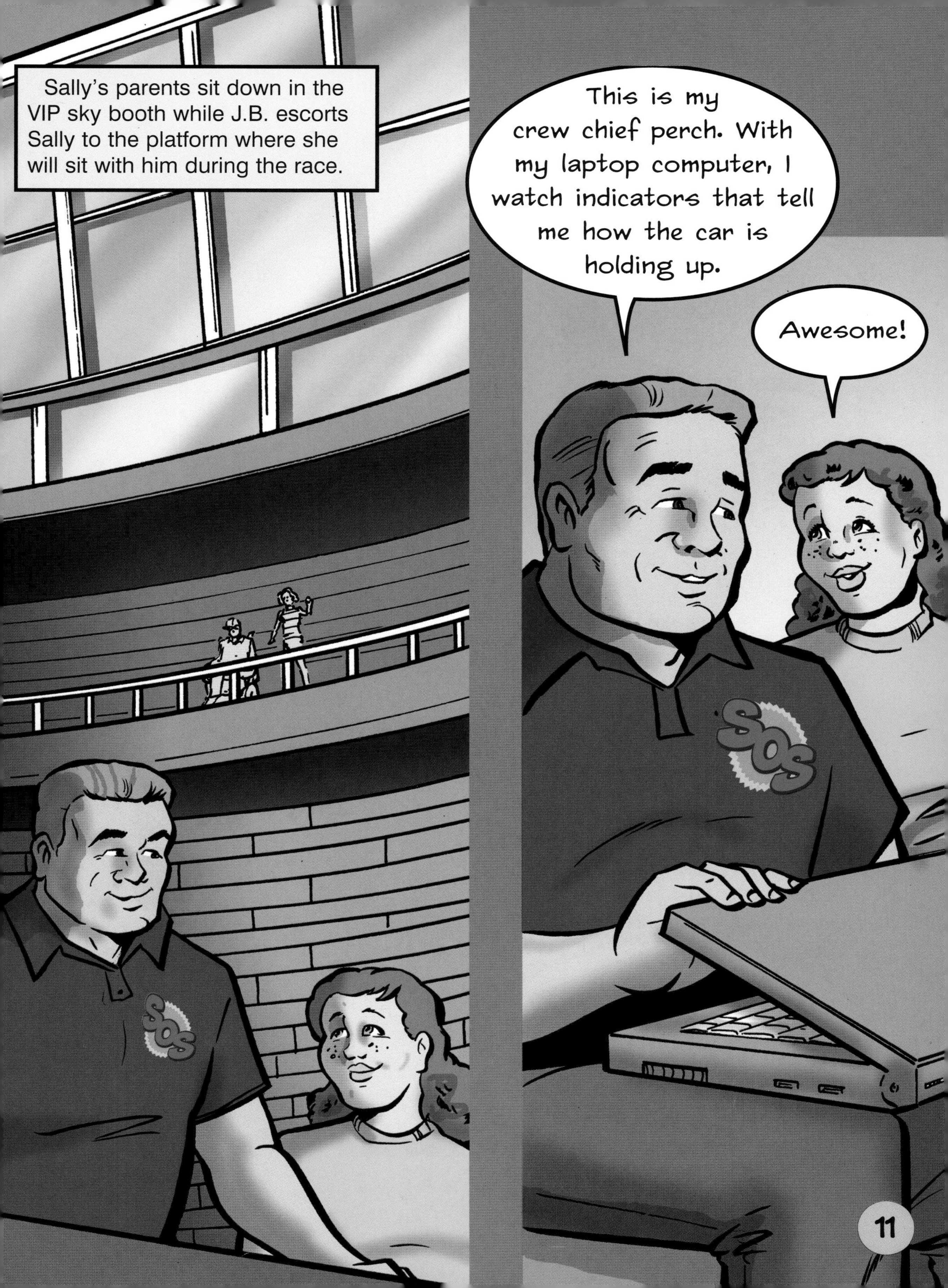
Sally's parents sit down in the VIP sky booth while J.B. escorts Sally to the platform where she will sit with him during the race.
This is my crew chief perch. With my laptop computer, I watch indicators that tell me how the car is holding up.
Awesome!
SOS
SOS

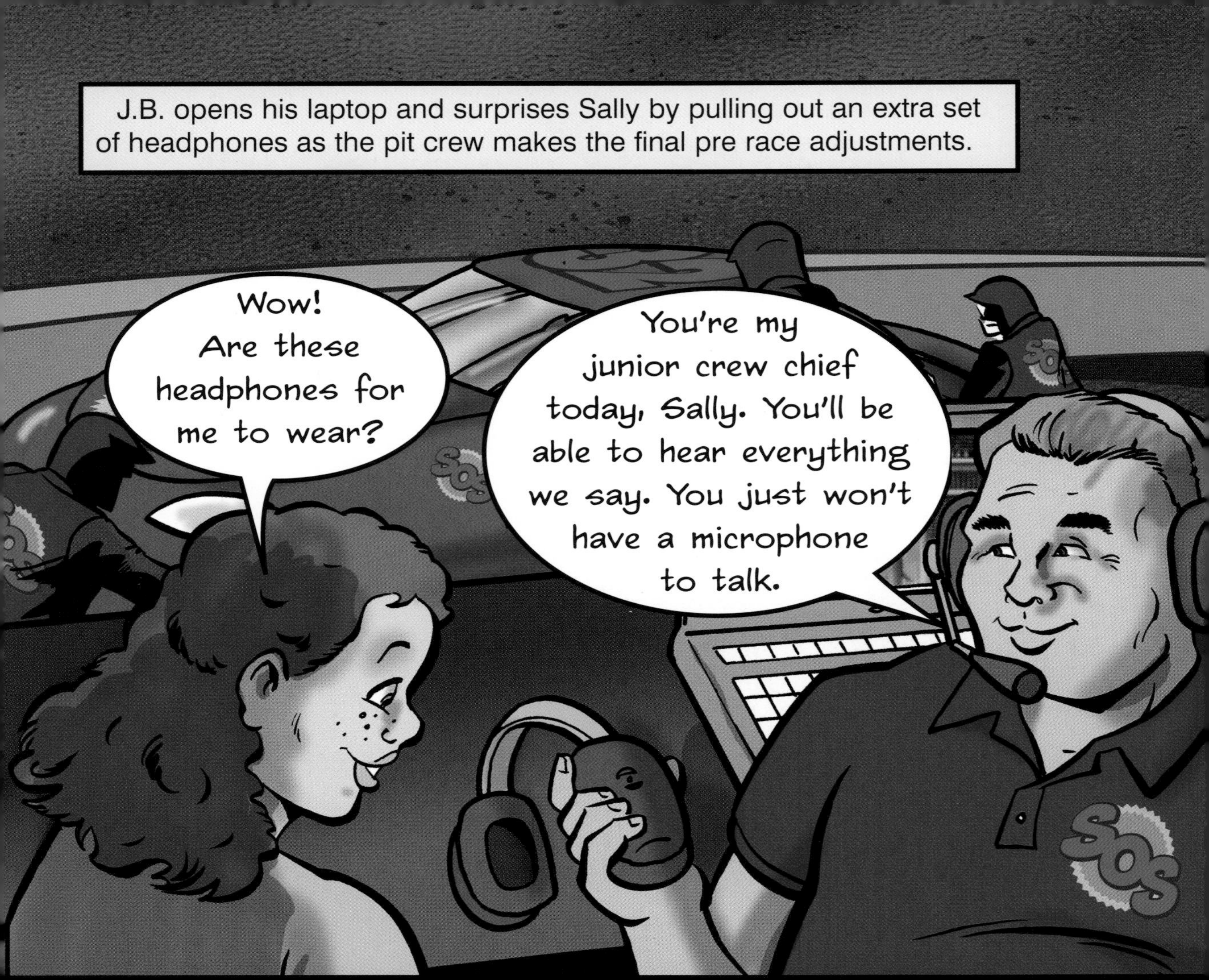
J.B. opens his laptop and surprises Sally by pulling out an extra set of headphones as the pit crew makes the final pre race adjustments.
Wow! Are these headphones for me to wear?
You're my junior crew chief today, Sally. You'll be able to hear everything we say. You just won't have a microphone to talk.

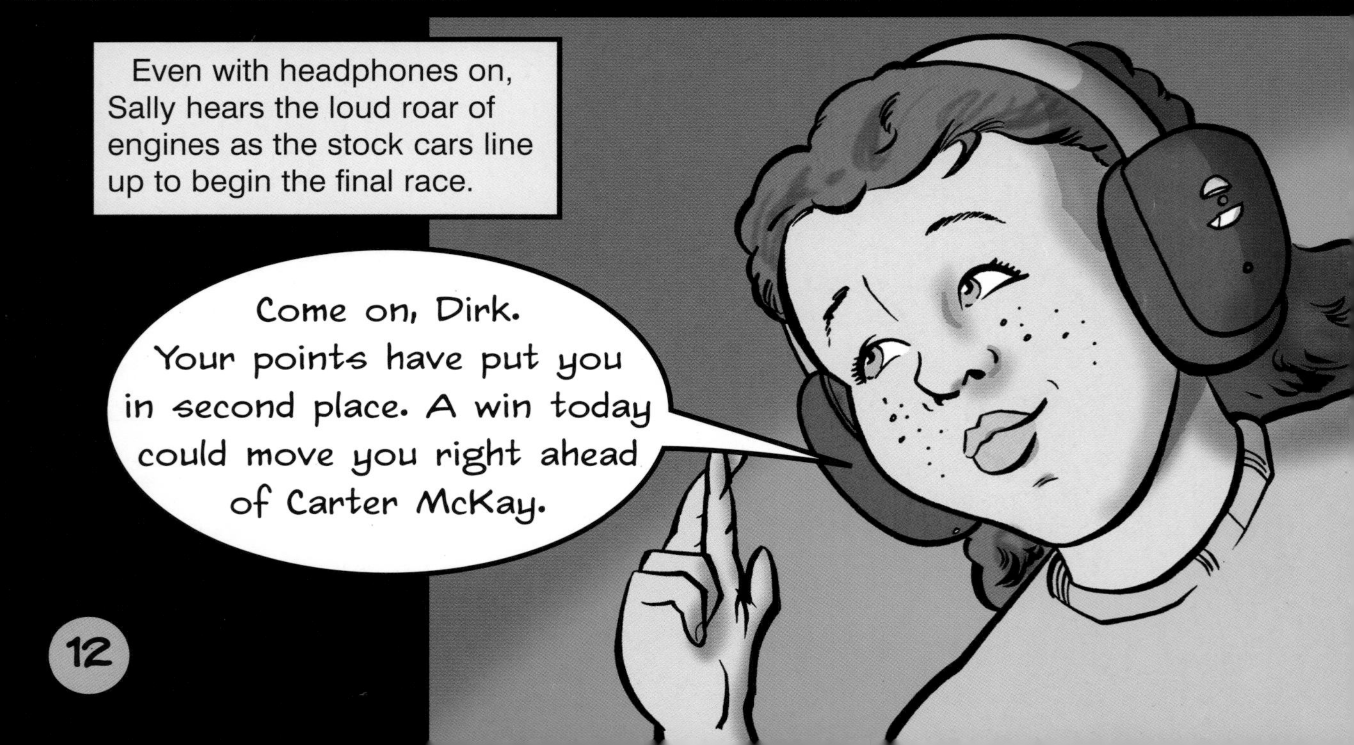
Even with headphones on, Sally hears the loud roar of engines as the stock cars line up to begin the final race.
Come on, Dirk. Your points have put you in second place. A win today could move you right ahead of Carter McKay.

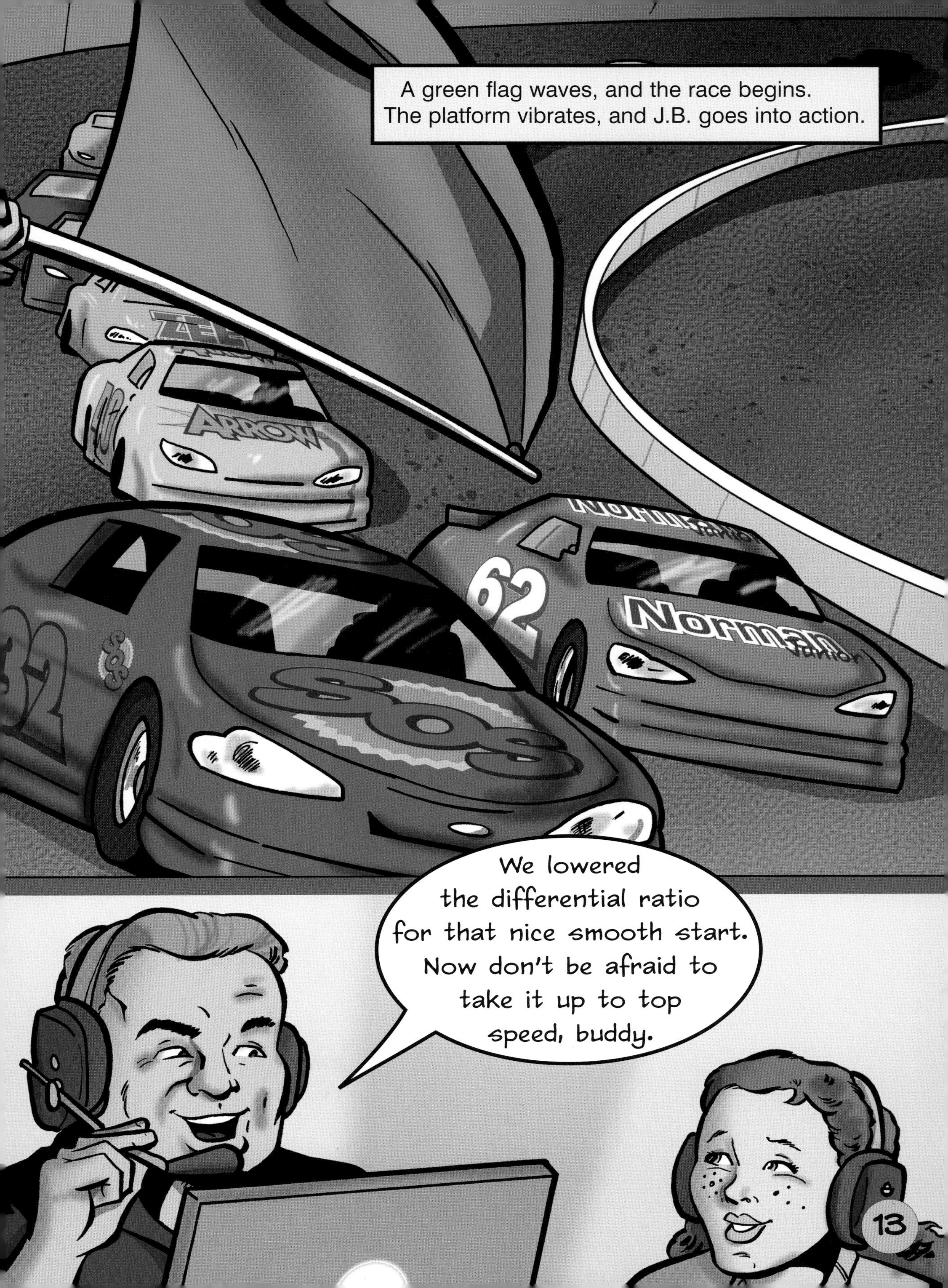
A green flag waves, and the race begins. The platform vibrates, and J.B. goes into action.
ARROW
62
Norman Junior
32
SOS
We lowered the differential ratio for that nice smooth start. Now don't be afraid to take it up to top speed, buddy.

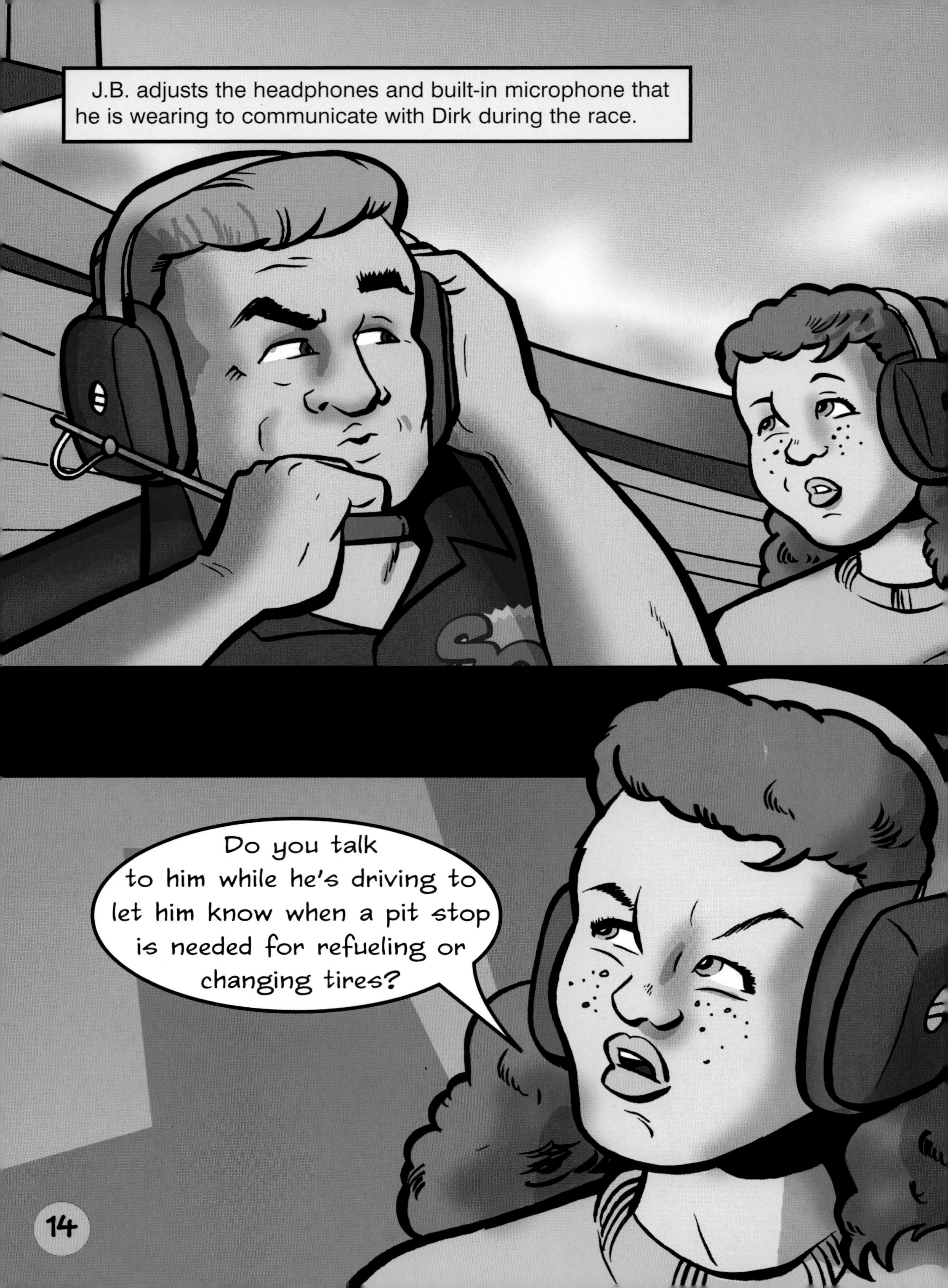
J.B. adjusts the headphones and built-in microphone that he is wearing to communicate with Dirk during the race.
Do you talk to him while he's driving to let him know when a pit stop is needed for refueling or changing tires?

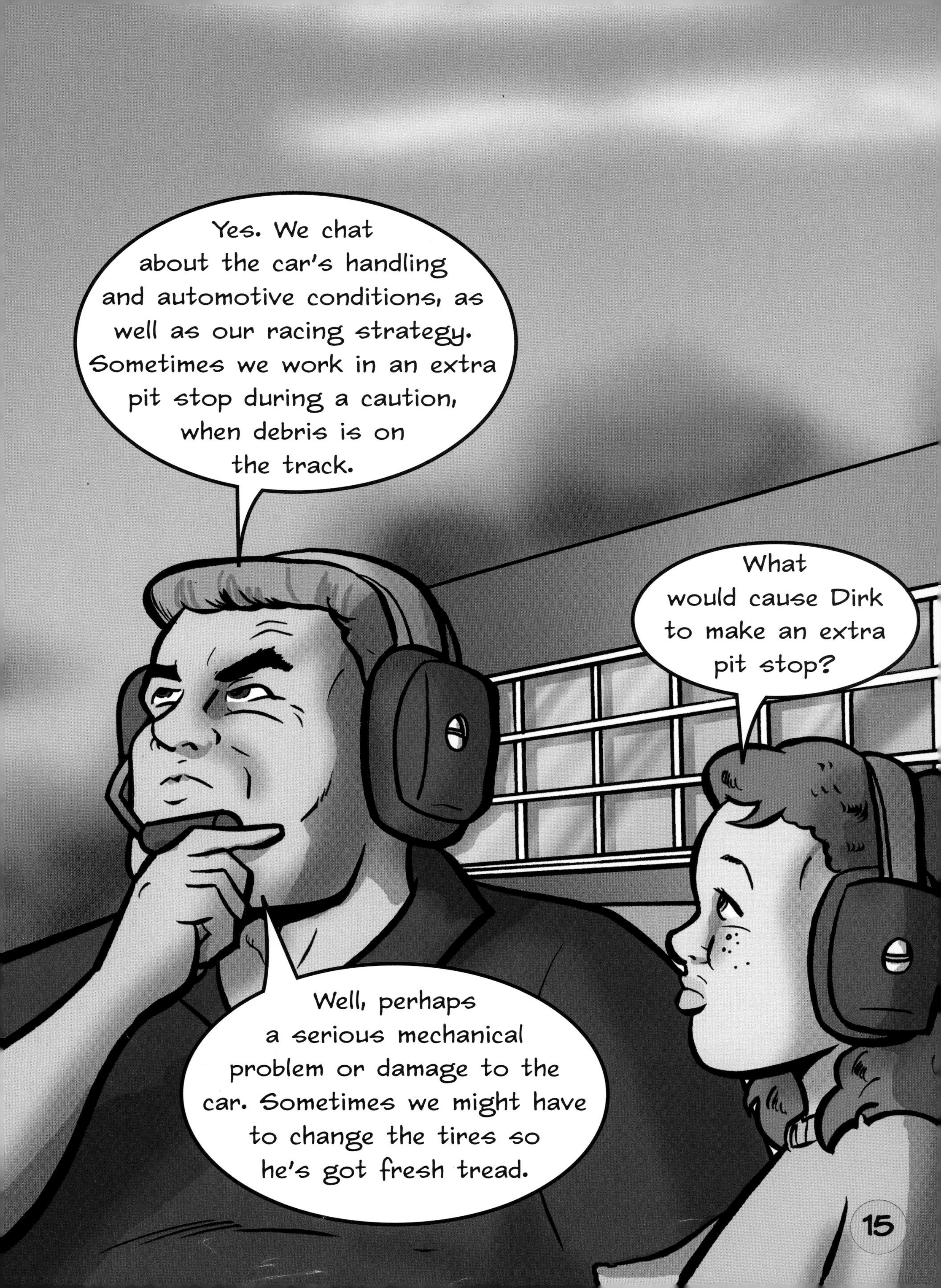
Yes. We chat about the car's handling and automotive conditions, as well as our racing strategy. Sometimes we work in an extra pit stop during a caution, when debris is on the track.
What would cause Dirk to make an extra pit stop?
Well, perhaps a serious mechanical problem or damage to the car. Sometimes we might have to change the tires so he's got fresh tread.

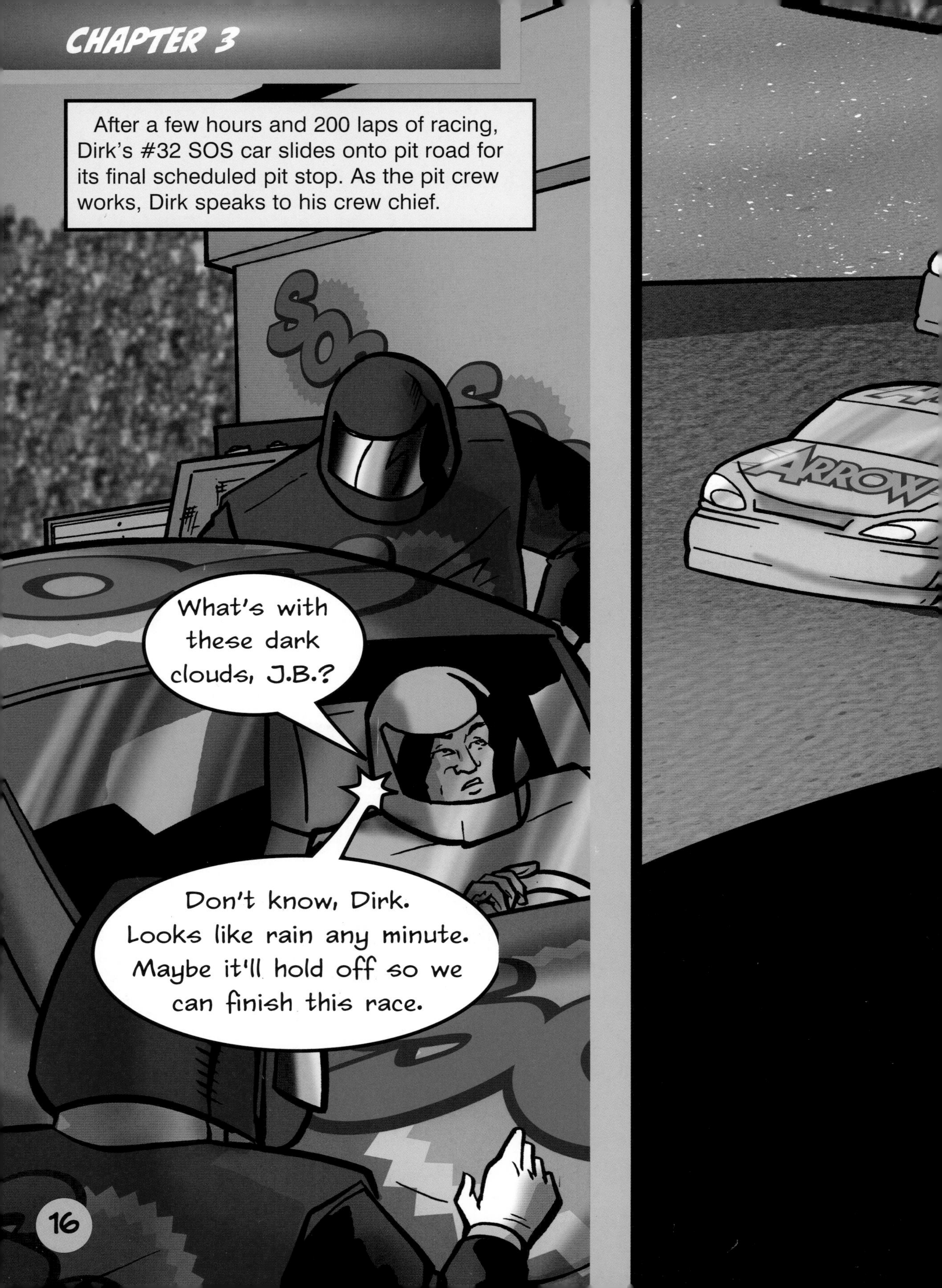
CHAPTER 3
After a few hours and 200 laps of racing, Dirk's #32 SOS car slides onto pit road for its final scheduled pit stop. As the pit crew works, Dirk speaks to his crew chief.
What's with these dark clouds, J.B.?
Don't know, Dirk. Looks like rain any minute. Maybe it'll hold off so we can finish this race.
ARROW

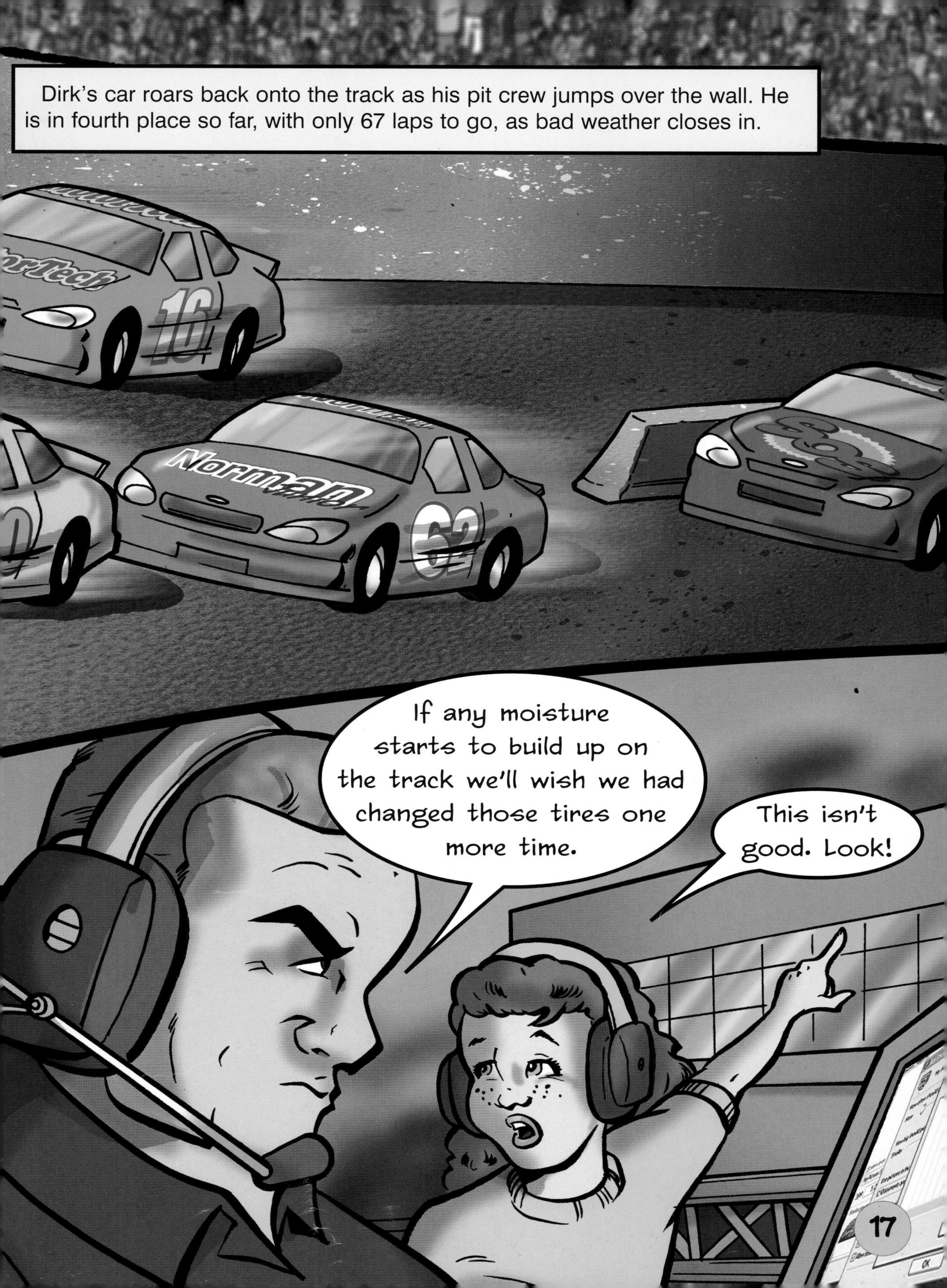
Dirk's car roars back onto the track as his pit crew jumps over the wall. He is in fourth place so far, with only 67 laps to go, as bad weather closes in.
If any moisture starts to build up on the track we'll wish we had changed those tires one more time.
This isn't good. Look!

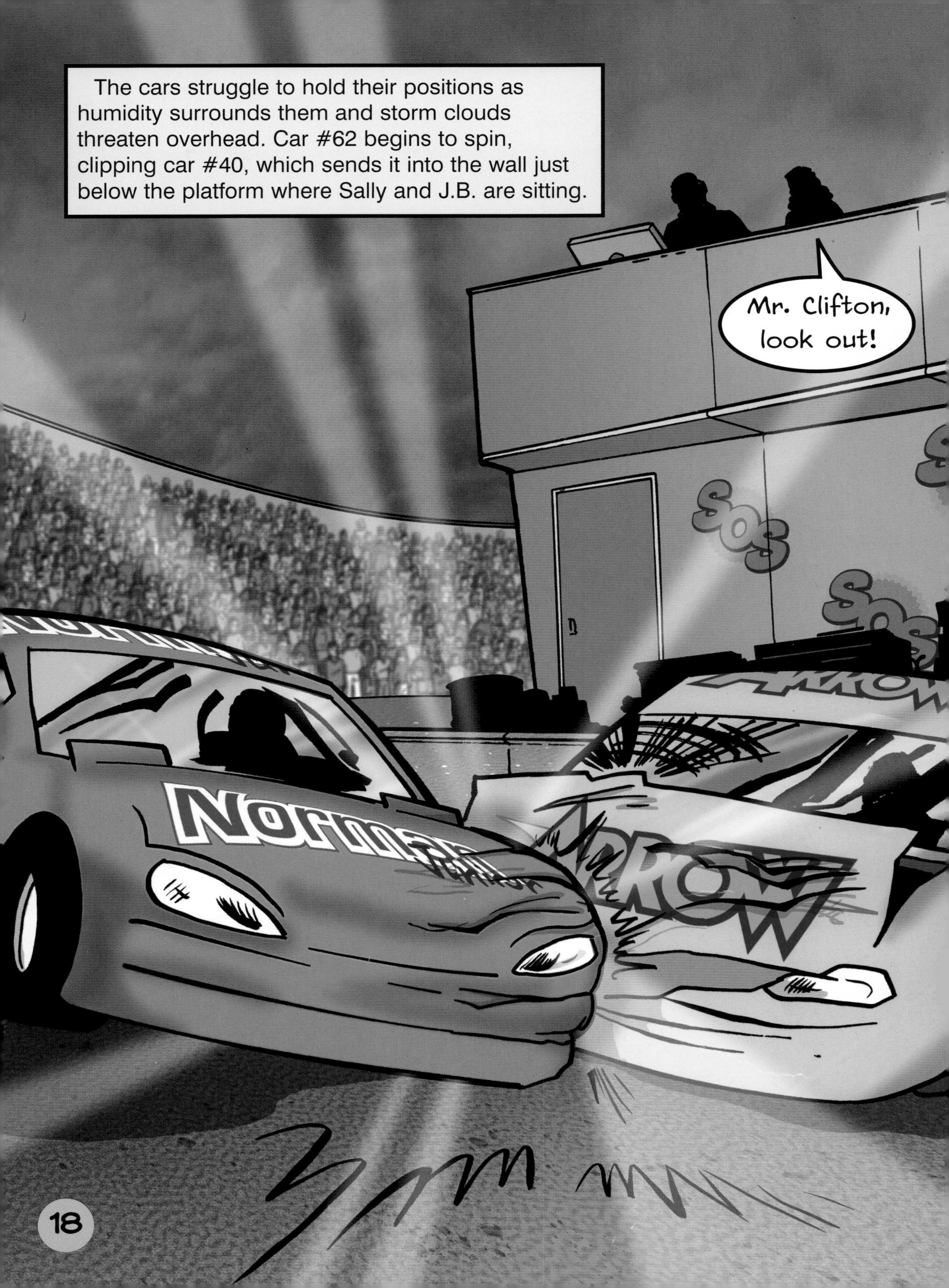
The cars struggle to hold their positions as humidity surrounds them and storm clouds threaten overhead. Car #62 begins to spin, clipping car #40, which sends it into the wall just below the platform where Sally and J.B. are sitting.
Mr. Clifton, look out!
SOS
SOS
Norman
ARROW

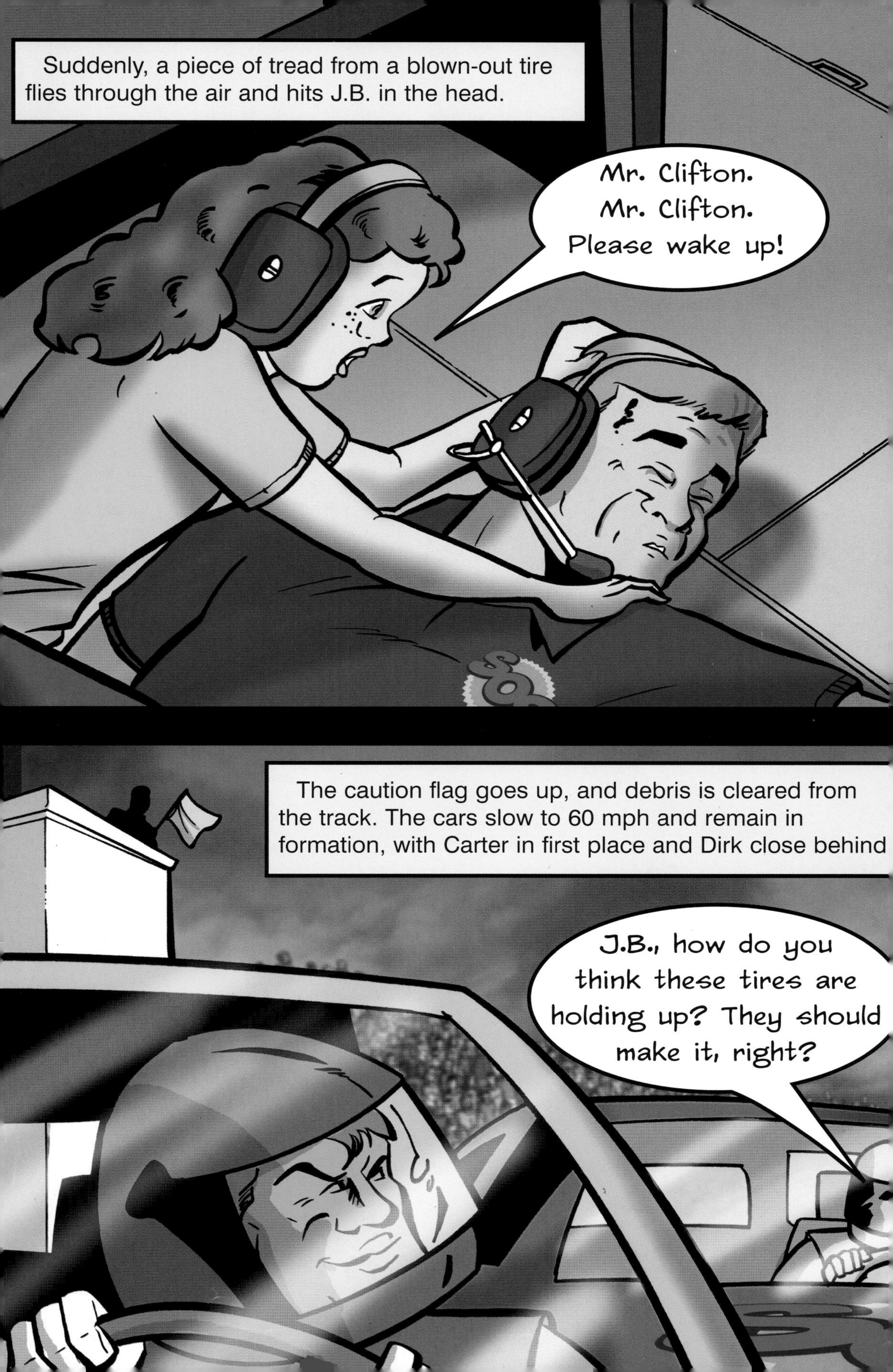
Suddenly, a piece of tread from a blown-out tire flies through the air and hits J.B. in the head.
Mr. Clifton. Mr. Clifton. Please wake up!
The caution flag goes up, and debris is cleared from the track. The cars slow to 60 mph and remain in formation, with Carter in first place and Dirk close behind
J.B., how do you think these tires are holding up? They should make it, right?

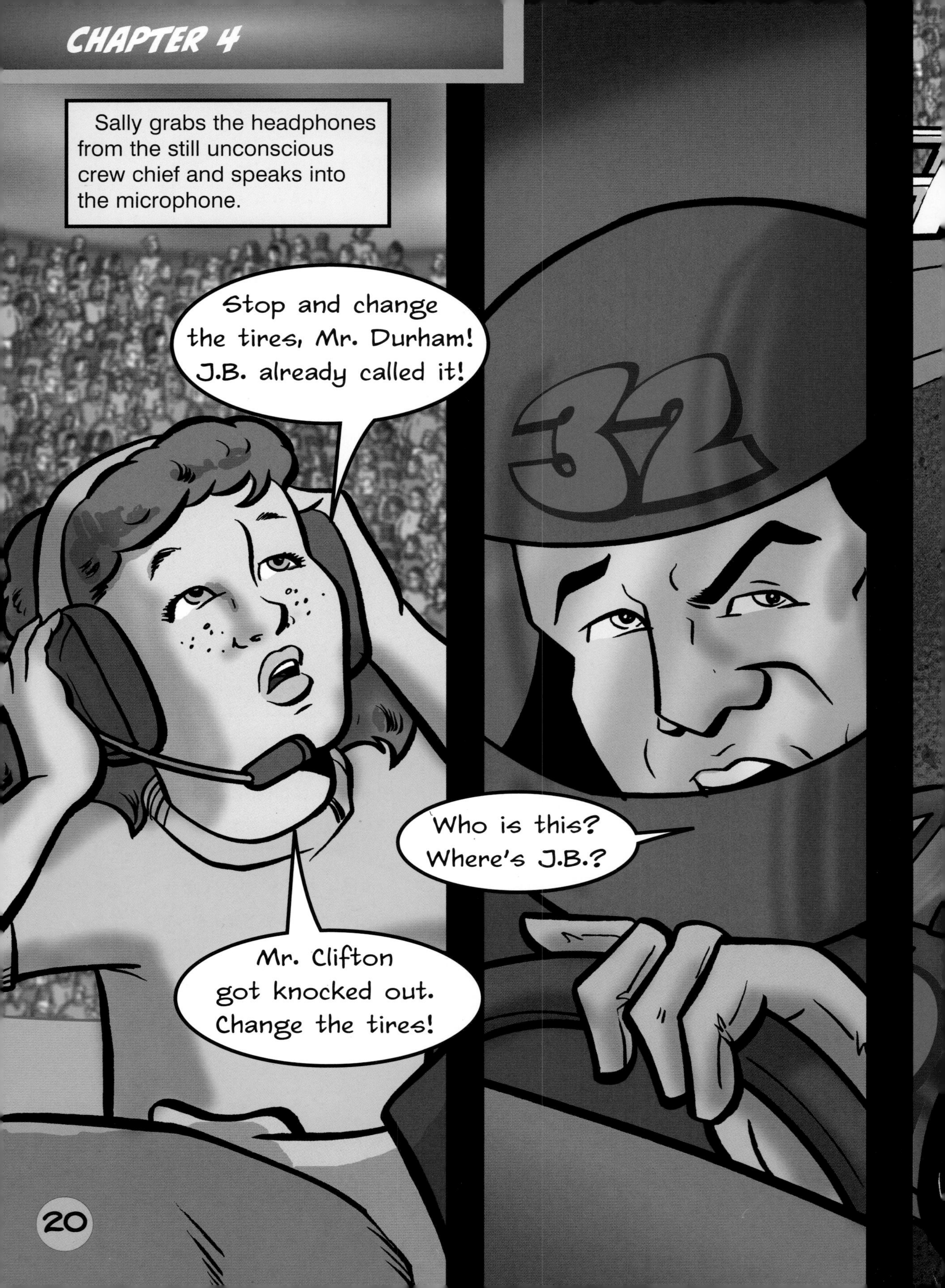
CHAPTER 4
Sally grabs the headphones from the still unconscious crew chief and speaks into the microphone.
Stop and change the tires, Mr. Durham! J.B. already called it!
32
Who is this? Where's J.B.?
Mr. Clifton got knocked out. Change the tires!

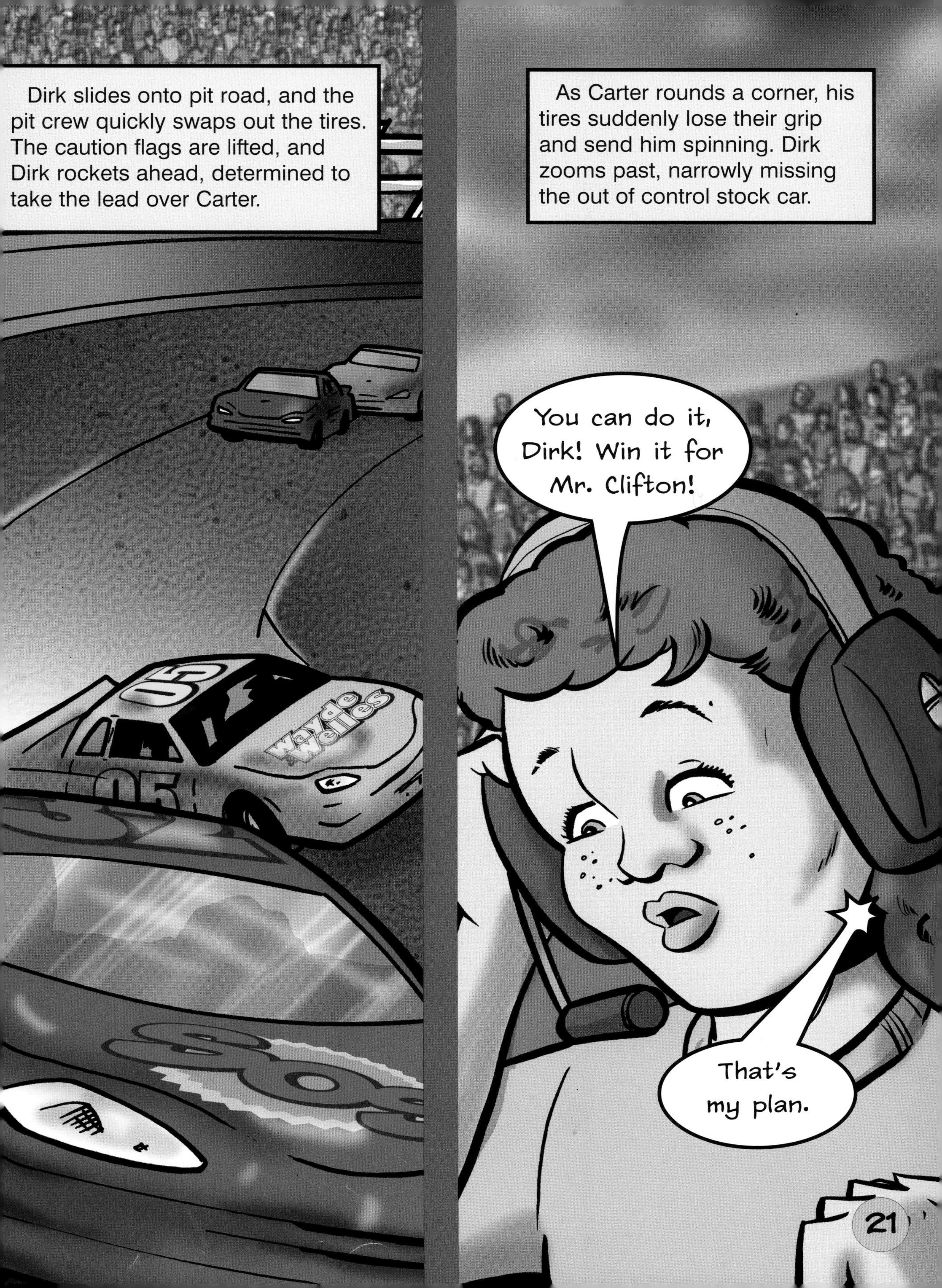
Dirk slides onto pit road, and the pit crew quickly swaps out the tires. The caution flags are lifted, and Dirk rockets ahead, determined to take the lead over Carter.
As Carter rounds a corner, his tires suddenly lose their grip and send him spinning. Dirk zooms past, narrowly missing the out of control stock car.
You can do it, Dirk! Win it for Mr. Clifton!
That's my plan.

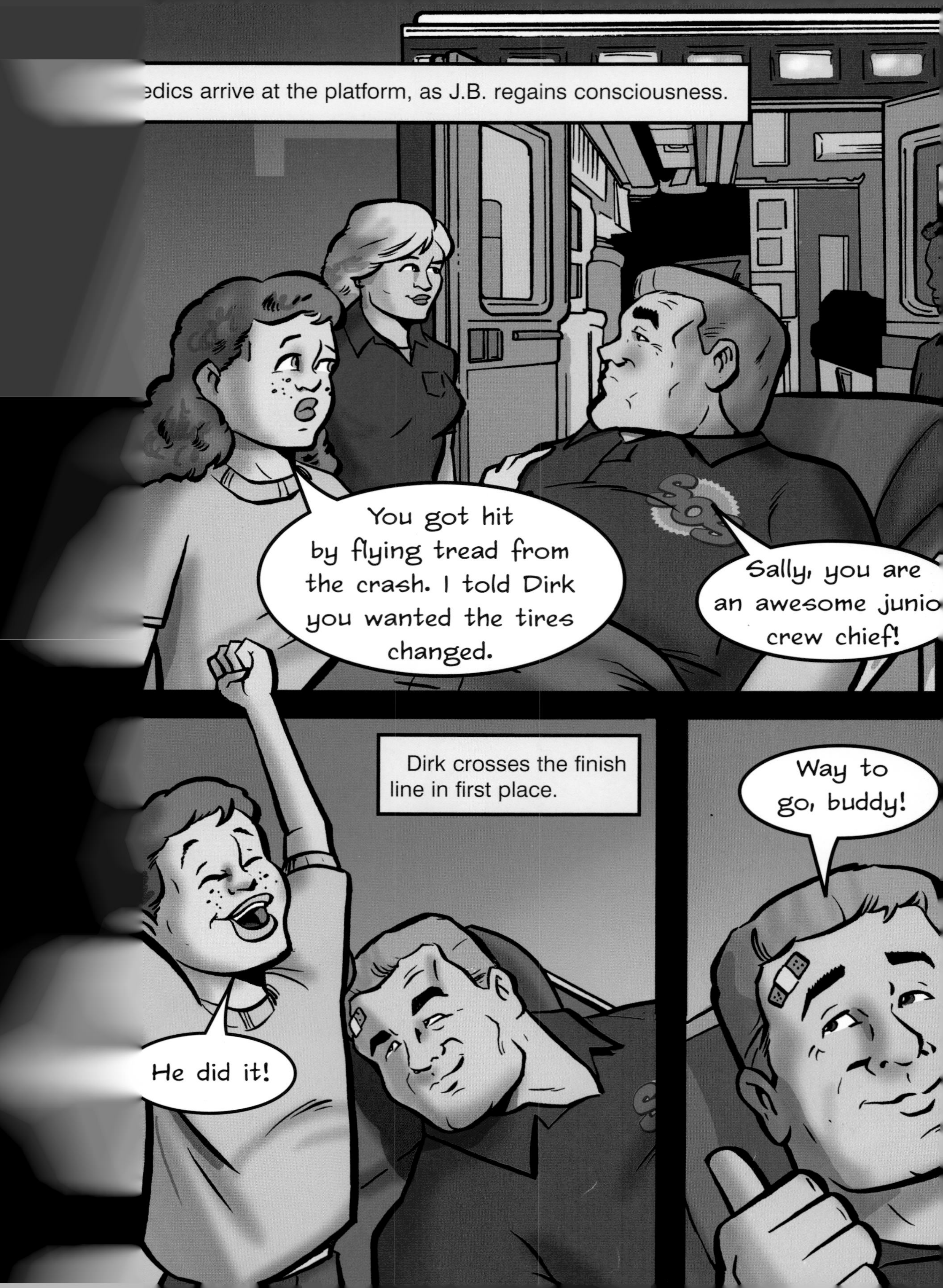
edics arrive at the platform, as J.B. regains consciousness.
You got hit by flying tread from the crash. I told Dirk you wanted the tires changed.
Sally, you are an awesome junio crew chief!
Dirk crosses the finish line in first place.
He did it!
Way to go, buddy!

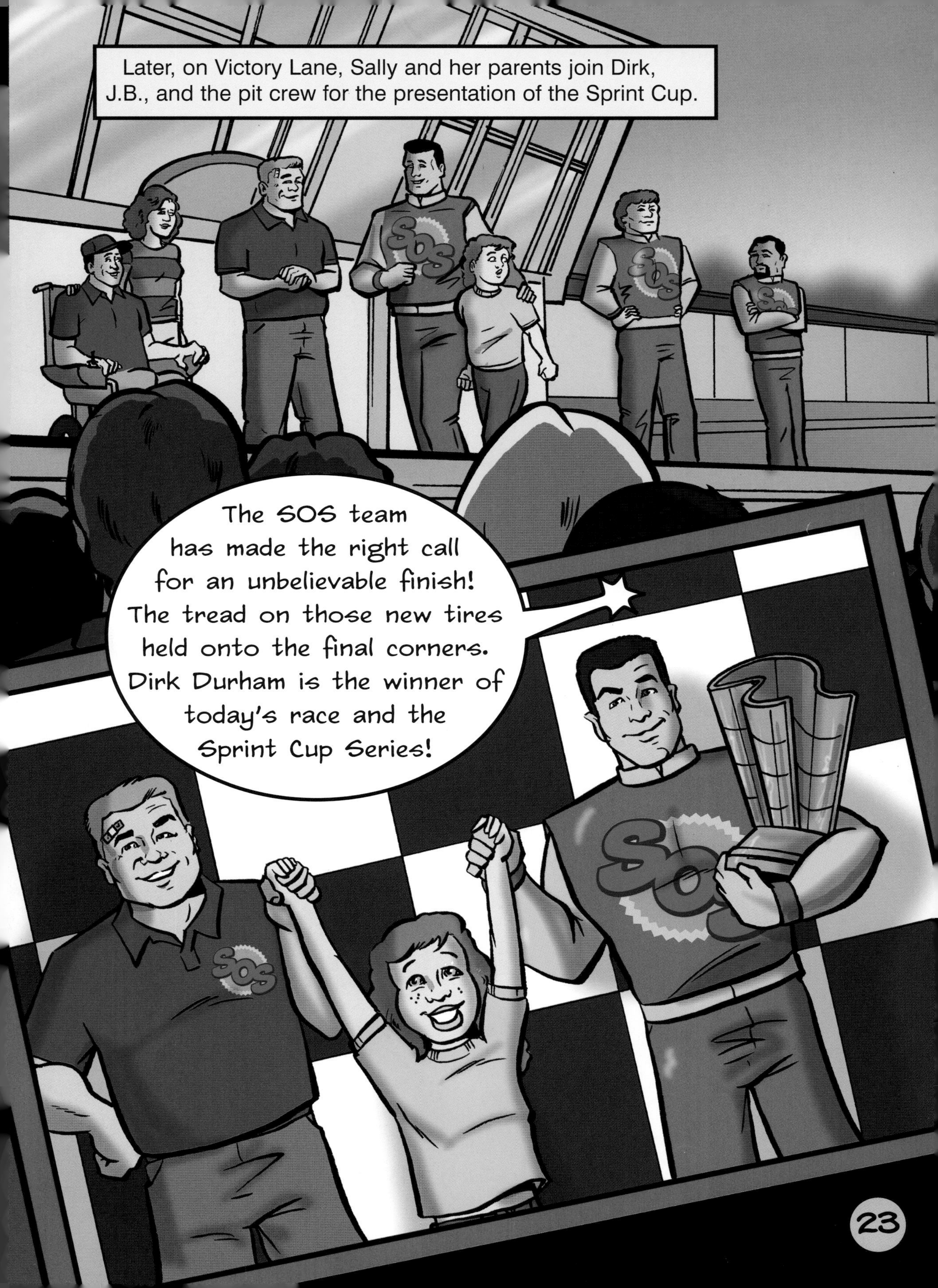
Later, on Victory Lane, Sally and her parents join Dirk, J.B., and the pit crew for the presentation of the Sprint Cup.
The SOS team has made the right call for an unbelievable finish! The tread on those new tires held onto the final corners. Dirk Durham is the winner of today's race and the Sprint Cup Series!
SOS

CHAPTER 5

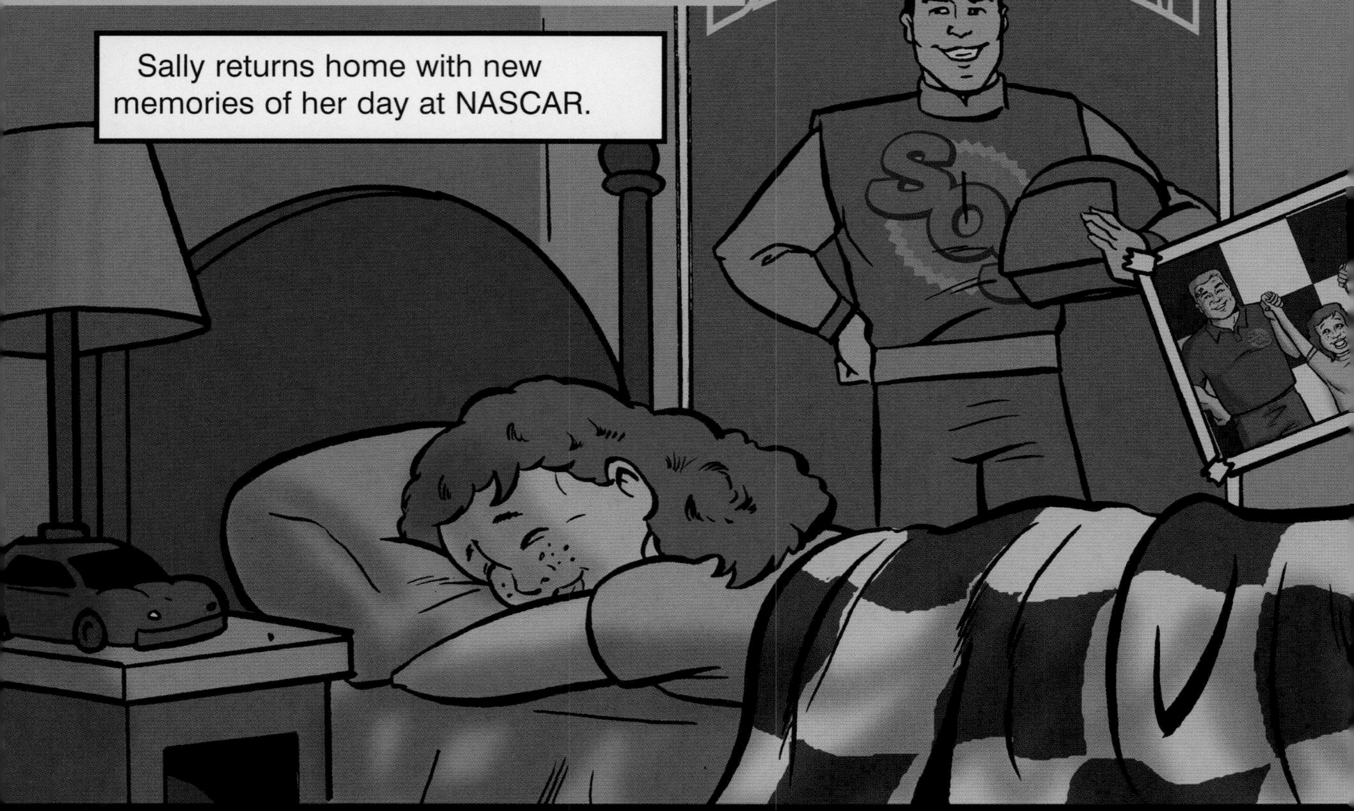
Sally returns home with new memories of her day at NASCAR.

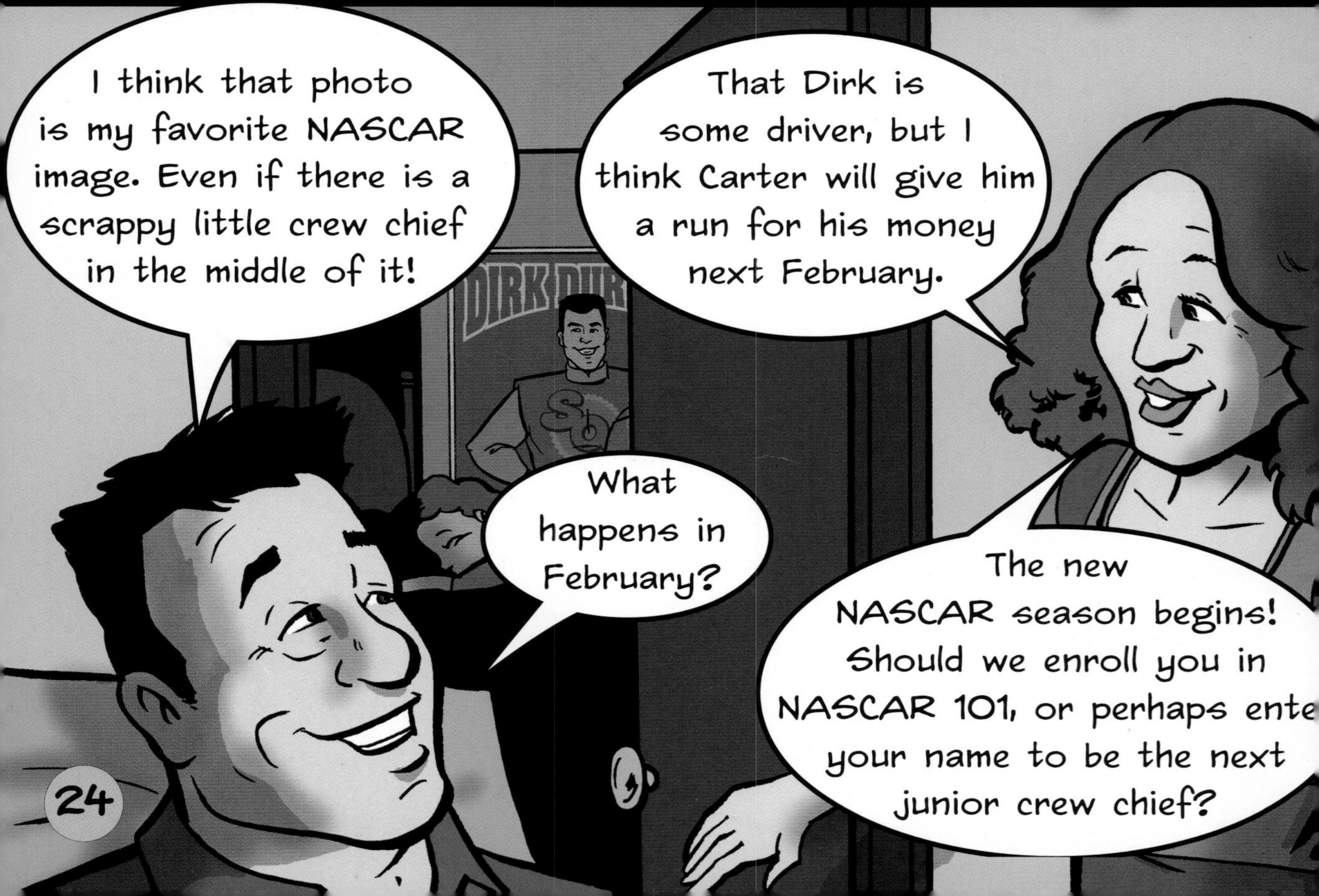
I think that photo is my favorite NASCAR image. Even if there is a scrappy little crew chief in the middle of it!
That Dirk is some driver, but I think Carter will give him a run for his money next February.
What happens in February?
The new NASCAR season begins! Should we enroll you in NASCAR 101, or perhaps ente your name to be the next junior crew chief?

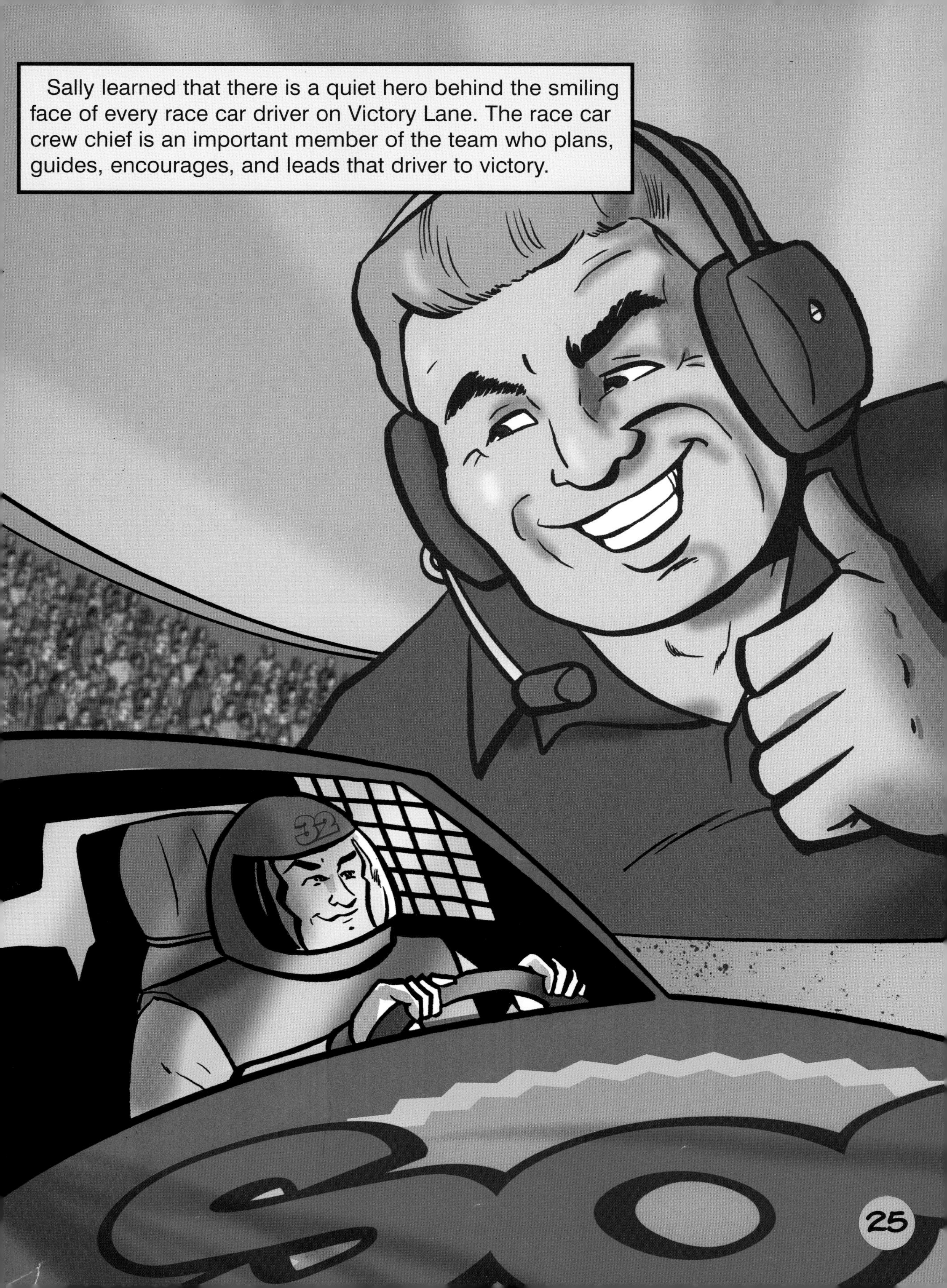
Sally learned that there is a quiet hero behind the smiling face of every race car driver on Victory Lane. The race car crew chief is an important member of the team who plans, guides, encourages, and leads that driver to victory.
32

A Crew Chief's Job is Never Done

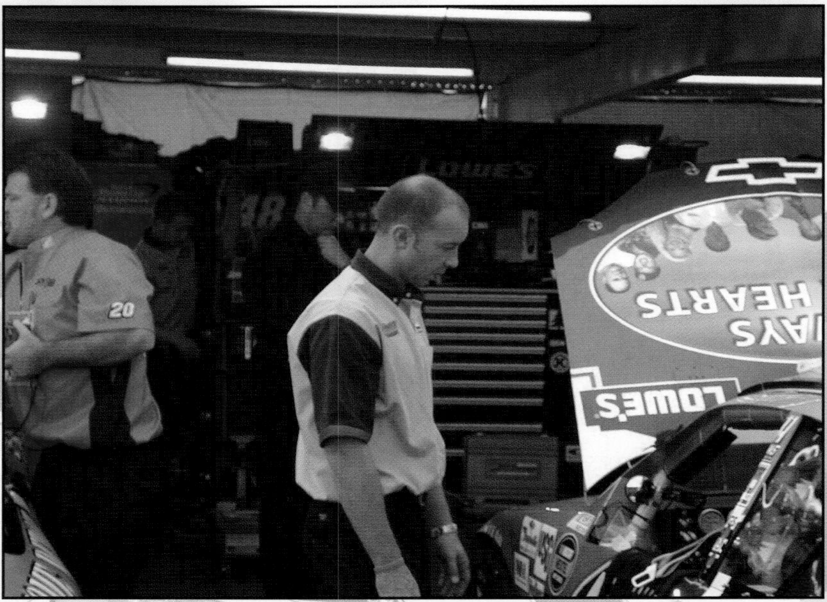
20
LOWE'S

Chad Knaus, one of the top crew chiefs, is involved in every aspect of a race.

While drivers are the focus of attention at races, it's the crew chief who manages the overall performance of the racing team. The crew chief is like a football head coach or baseball manager. He instructs both the driver and pit crew during the race.

The list of a crew chief's responsibilities is a long one. He is involved in every aspect of the race car's preparation, the readiness and performance of the pit crew, and of course, the strategy the driver uses during the race.

In fact, some crew chiefs say the race car is theirs, and the driver is merely hired to drive it. The crew chief, driver, and pit crew are in frequent communication during the race, but the crew chief is in charge.

Tire changers use air guns to remove lug nuts from the tires in order to change them as quickly as possible.

Pit Crew Safety

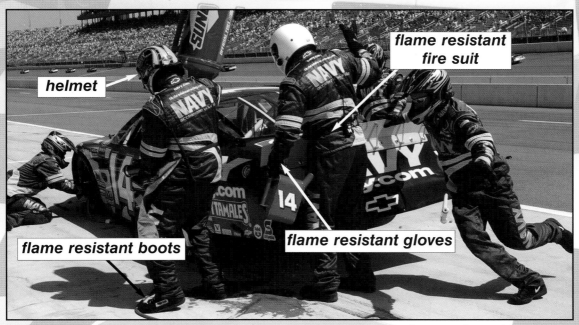

helmet

flame resistant fire suit

flame resistant boots

flame resistant gloves

Under all the other necessary clothing, crew members in charge of gas have to wear flame resistant underwear on the top and bottom.

Pit Stops

Seven crew members are allowed over the wall during a routine pit stop. Each member has a specific job assignment. The members fill the car with gas and change all four tires in about 13 to 15 seconds!

The pit crew consists of the rear and front tire carriers, rear and front tire changers, **jack man**, gas man, and gas catch man. The gas man and gas catch man work to refuel the car. The tire carriers carry tires over the walls, while the jack man elevates the car. Once the car is elevated, the tire changers go into action. Sometimes an eighth pit crew member is allowed over the wall to clean the car's windshield.

A successful pit stop is well-planned and fast.

States that Host NASCAR Sprint Cup Series

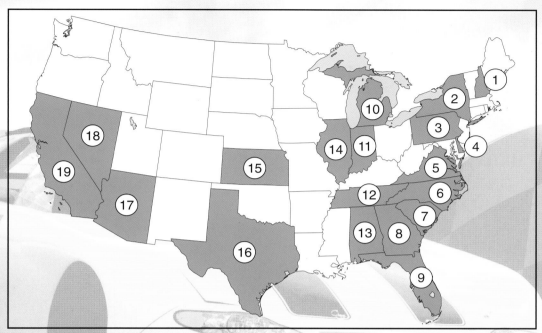

The first race of NASCAR's season is the Daytona 500. The race is 500 miles (805 kilometers) long, or 200 laps around the track.

Number	Location	Number	Location
1	Loudon, New Hampshire	11	Speedway, Indiana
2	Watkins Glen, New York	12	Bristol, Tennessee
3	Long Pond, Pennsylvania	13	Talladega, Alabama
4	Dover, Delaware	14	Joliet, Illinois
5	Martinsville, Virginia	15	Kansas City, Kansas
	Richmond, Virginia	16	Fort Worth, Texas
6	Concord, North Carolina	17	Avondale, Arizona
7	Darlington, South Carolina	18	Las Vegas, Nevada
8	Hampton, Georgia	19	Fontana, California
9	Daytona Beach, Florida		Sonoma, California
	Homestead, Florida		
10	Brooklyn, Michigan		

Glossary

caution flag (KAW-shun FLAG): A yellow flag that requires drivers to slow down due to a hazard on the track.

debris (du-BREE): The remains of something broken down or destroyed.

differential ratio (DIF-ur-en-chul RAY-shee-oh): The differential ratio determines how fast the engine will rev at different speeds.

jack man (JAK MAN): The crew member who raises the car so the tires can be changed.

NASCAR (NAS-kar): An acronym which stands for the National Association of Stock Car Auto Racing. It is the largest organization for car racing in the United States.

Sprint Cup Series (SPRINT KUP SI-rez): The top racing competition in NASCAR. It consists of 36 races throughout the United States.

stock car (STOK KAR): A race car that has the same basic structure as a commercially made assembly-line car.

tread (TRED): The outside of a tire that helps prevent the tires from slipping or sliding on the pavement.

Victory Lane (VIK-tu-ree LAN): The spot on each racetrack's infield where the race winner parks for the celebration.

Websites

www.sae.org/exdomains/awim

www.stockcarscience.com

www.aptv.org/PIF/racecar.asp

Index

About the Author

Susan Koehler is a teacher and a writer who lives in Tallahassee, Florida. As a child, she loved reading mysteries. She liked books so much that she gave up her recess time in elementary school to work in the school library. Beyond the pages of books, she enjoyed listening to stories about the colorful, real-life experiences of her parents and older siblings. Now she lives in a busy house filled with books, animals, and very funny children.

About the Artist

After graduating from the Joe Kubert School of Cartoon and Graphic Art, Thom Zahler began his ten-year career as a caricaturist at an amusement park. Later, Zahler began drawing cartoons and other silly pictures for clients such as the Cleveland Indians, the Colorado Rockies, and the Rock and Roll Hall of Fame. He has also worked for Marvel Comics, DC Comics, and Warner Brothers International. Zahler currently writes and draws Love and Capes, a romantic comedy comic book. Zahler lives in Timberlake, Ohio. He works from his house, frequently in his pajamas, and always with a cup of coffee.